The Bee Attitudes

And 5 More Extraordinary Plays For Ordinary Days

Frank Ramirez

CSS Publishing Company, Inc., Lima, Ohio

THE BEE ATTITUDES

Copyright © 2007 by
CSS Publishing Company, Inc.
Lima, Ohio

The original purchaser may photocopy material in this publication for use as it was intended (worship material for worship use; educational material for classroom use; dramatic material for staging or production). No additional permission is required from the publisher for such copying by the original purchaser only. Inquiries should be addressed to: Permissions, CSS Publishing Company, Inc., 517 South Main Street, Lima, Ohio 45804.

Scripture quotations are from the New Revised Standard Version of the Bible, copyright 1989 by the Division of Christian Education of the National Council of the Churches of Christ in the USA. Used by permission.

For more information about CSS Publishing Company resources, visit our website at www.csspub.com or email us at custserv@csspub.com or call (800) 241-4056.

Cover design by Frank Ramirez and Barbara Spencer — Photo used by permission
ISBN-13: 979-0-7880-2435-0
ISBN-10: 0-7880-2435-3   PRINTED IN U.S.A.

Dedicated to
Dr. Gradyon F. Snyder,
"Grady"
Scholar, Dean, Professor, Mentor,
Writer, Translator, Churchman,
Friend
Hail Fellow! Well Met!

And the Word was made Flesh and Tented among us!

Writ In Rome About A Tower

That unknown shepherd called from Hermes — from
Some lady he called Rhoda and that she
Had left a message that was writ in Rome
About a Tower built upon the sea.

That was it! That Rome was home to Rhoda.
What else? There was another name I'm certain.
And both was sure when you was young you knowda,
— a sibyl something scribbled on the curtain.

Oh well. Forget it. That was unimportant.
What I remembered best and be assured
That this is on the level and no portent,
But coin of *koine*, Logos from the Word:

The edifice, from Christ-perfected stone,
Includes a brick that over years you've won.

Table Of Contents

Introduction	7
The Bee Attitudes	9
Witnesses To The Light	15
Holy Water	29
Holy Ground	45
Considerable Provocation	65
Noah's New Ark	79

Introduction

At the heart of our faith as Christians is the belief that the Word was made flesh and dwelt among us. The Incarnation, the presence of Jesus as Immanuel, is what defines us. When we ask ourselves the question, "What would Jesus do?" when we attempt to walk in his steps, when we sing, "He the great example is and pattern for me," we confess that in our own way we try to become a little word made flesh, to reveal a little something about Jesus in the manner of our living.

Drama is an attempt to help words take on flesh and dwell in our midst. Despite the obvious connection between theater and our faith, there are some Christians who are not comfortable with drama. However, I've learned over the years that no matter what you do in worship, whether it's sing a new song, redecorate the altar, or stick with the same old hymns and prayers, someone will express dissatisfaction. Perhaps some of these problems come because we're looking at each other. The proper attitude in worship is to look toward God. The purpose of worship is to praise God.

The plays were written as one way to praise God in worship. They were generally created for specific occasions in the normal life of our congregation, the Everett (Pennsylvania) Church of the Brethren. They were all presented during worship services, page in hand, even when staged in a realistic fashion.

"The Bee Attitudes" came about because our children's choir was enjoying the songs they were learning but weren't too excited about an old play that went with them. "Holy Water" was written overnight when our youth leader confessed that the youth wanted a play, but didn't think I had enough time to write one. "Considerable Provocation" was written during a long weekend at the request of a denominational youth leader and was made available to all churches in our denomination. "Witnesses To The Light" is a response to some of the tiresome misinformation about Mary of Magdala, often called Mary Magdalene, that seems to resurface again and again over Christian history.

The characters of the Angels Marvelous, Wonderful, and Gabriel appear in other plays I've written that have been published by CSS, specifically "M.I.H. — Missing In Heaven" from the anthology, *Roll Back The Stone*, and also in *Gabriel's Horn*.

With the exception of "Witnesses To The Light," all were written for children and for youth. Some folks say that the young people are the church of tomorrow. I say that the youth and children are the church of today, and should be invited to participate regularly in worship as scripture readers, worship leaders, musicians, and speakers.

I hope all who produce and perform these plays will feel free to make changes to suit their own situations. I pray that regardless of whether they are read, or exquisitely performed, that God will be praised with tears and laughter in all our churches. True union comes from our common confession that Jesus is the risen Lord. Most everything else is just window dressing.

Frank Ramirez

The Bee Attitudes

Cast
    Crystal
    Doris
    Garrison
    Vanessa
    Olivia
    Taylor
    Morgan
    Director
    Piano Player

Props
    Table with a stack of books in the middle of it
    Posters laying on the table
    Piano
    Large, heavy book
    Costumes for children (bee costumes or headpieces with antennae)

Production Note

This particular play was written for a children's choir that was practicing particular numbers at the time. The musical numbers listed can certainly be changed according to the talents and repertoire of the group of children who are performing this play.

(All the students enter, wearing either coverings that are striped like honeybees, or headpieces with bee antennae, or both. They take their places.)

Crystal: Are you ready, everyone?

Doris: Ready!

Crystal: Then let's show our Bee Attitudes!

Children: Buzz! Buzz! Buzz! *(circle with their arms extended, then cross in a figure eight pattern, then line up again)*

Garrison: I'm tired!

Vanessa: Being a Bee is hard work.

Olivia: Maybe that's why all the Bees have Bee Attitudes.

Taylor: This is not helping my hair *one* bit!

Morgan: Are you sure this is what our director means by Bee Attitudes?

Taylor: What else could she mean? She said we were going to sing about the Bee Attitudes.

Crystal: And one thing is for sure — Bee Attitudes must be very good, or she wouldn't want us to sing about them.

Morgan: Well, my dad keeps bees, and sometimes bees have very bad attitudes.

Doris: Yeah. I hope I don't get stung!

Vanessa: Well, let's try to get some good Bee Attitudes before our director gets here. Let's practice one of our songs.

Garrison: Okay, and if Bee Attitudes are supposed to be good, then we ought to be happy all the time.

(Children sing "Happy All The Time." At the end, Olivia runs off stage.)

Doris: What a good song. It tells us to be happy and glad.

Crystal: That's not always easy to do, but I remember hearing in Sunday school that ancient prophets were persecuted, too.

Morgan: I don't know. I can't imagine the bees I know singing that song.

Olivia: *(enters, carrying a big, heavy book)* I had an idea. The Bee Attitudes are supposed to be in the Bible. Maybe they're in this book.

Taylor: Where did you get that book?

Olivia: *(slams it down on the table)* From the pastor's office.

Crystal: Do you think he'll miss it?

Garrison: No, he has lots of books.

Vanessa: Yeah, I'll bet his wife is very happy that we borrowed one of his books. She says he has too many.

Morgan: Wow! This is a very big book. Let's see what it says about Bee Attitudes.

Crystal: *(points into book)* Look! It says the Bee Attitudes are something Jesus said.

Doris: Yes. Bee Attitudes are good attitudes.

Taylor: Oh, look. Jesus said, "Seek ye first the kingdom of God!"

Vanessa: Don't we know a song with that title?

Olivia: Yes, we do!

(Children sing "Seek Ye First.")

Morgan: This book actually has the Bee Attitudes. Let's read them.

(As each child reads a Beatitude, he or she also picks up a poster from the table, which has the Beatitude printed on the front and holds it up.)

Morgan: Blessed are the poor in spirit, for theirs is the kingdom of heaven.

Crystal: Blessed are those who mourn, for they will be comforted.

Olivia: Blessed are the meek, for they will inherit the earth.

Garrison: Blessed are those who hunger and thirst for righteousness, for they will be filled.

Taylor: Blessed are the merciful, for they will receive mercy.

Doris: Blessed are the pure in heart, for they will see God.

Vanessa: Blessed are the peacemakers, for they will be called children of God.

Morgan and Crystal: Blessed are those who are persecuted for righteousness' sake, for theirs is the kingdom of heaven.

Doris, Vanessa, and Taylor: Blessed are you when people revile you and persecute you and utter all kinds of evil against you falsely on my account.

Garrison and Olivia: Rejoice and be glad, for your reward is great in heaven, for in the same way they persecuted the prophets who were before you.

Morgan: I get it! The Bee Attitudes teach us that people who are good and follow Jesus will be rewarded and go to heaven.

(Children sing "When I Get To Heaven.")

Doris: I wonder if it is hard to try to live by these Bee Attitudes.

Garrison: I'll bet it's hard sometimes to do the right thing.

Taylor: That's why Jesus told us that when we're down, to remember our reward.

(Children sing "When You're Down So Low.")

Crystal: I'm glad we borrowed this book from the pastor. It tells us that when we live our lives by the Bee Attitudes, even when times are tough, we can feel God's peace!

(Children sing "Peace Like A River.")

(Director and Piano Player enter. Piano Player sits down at the piano.)

Director: Hello, children! Sorry I'm late. Are you ready to practice?

Vanessa: Yes. We've already warmed up.

Director: Good. Now today we are going to learn more about the Beatitudes.

Piano Player: *(calls out from the piano)* What is a Beatitude anyway?

Director: I'll bet the children don't know.

Children: Yes, we do! Yes, we do!

Director: *(ignores them)* I remember that when I was little I got a D on my report card. Mom said it was because of my "poor attitude." She said I had to work really hard to do better on my report card the next time.

Morgan: I don't think that's it.

Doris: Try again!

Director: *(ignores them again)* I made sure I did all my homework and I raised my grade to a B. That made me think I had a B attitude!

Taylor: Good guess, but according to this book ...

Crystal: *(interrupts)* a Bee Attitude is a beautiful way of looking at God and life!

Olivia: Even when times are hard ...

Vanessa: *(interrupts)* we always remember that we can be happy and blessed!

Director: It sounds like all of you have been doing some research on your own! Well, let's get ready to sing our songs on the Beatitudes! That way, when our pastor preaches about the Beatitudes, we can sing about them.

Olivia: I don't think that's going to happen!

Director: Why not?

Morgan: Because we have his book!

Director: I'll see that he gets it back. In the meantime, let's sing about the way we feel when we live like Jesus!

(Children sing a reprise of "Happy All The Time.")

Witnesses To The Light: Mary of Magdala — I Have Seen The Lord!

Characters
  Angels
    Fantastic
    Marvelous
    Wonderful
    Gabriel
  Mary Of Magdala
  Joanna (wife of Chuza)

Props
  Script
  Angel costumes

Note
  This drama is based on Luke 8:1-3 and John 20:1-19.

Fantastic: Two minutes to airtime!

Marvelous: Hello! Hello, everybody! Has anyone seen Gabriel?

Fantastic: And you are?

Marvelous: Marvelous.

Fantastic: I'm sure you are.

Marvelous: No, I mean my name is Marvelous.

Fantastic: Fantastic.

Marvelous: Well, I like my name, too.

Fantastic: No, I mean, my name is Fantastic. And you're looking for?

Marvelous: Gabriel! Gabriel's supposed to be here.

Fantastic: Gabriel?

Marvelous: Gabriel's an angel.

Fantastic: Maybe you haven't noticed, but this place is crawling with angels. I'm an angel. You're an angel. We're all angels around here, except for the saints. This *is* heaven, after all.

Marvelous: It *was* heaven, until certain angels started throwing their weight around.

Fantastic: Pardon me?

Marvelous: Okay, you're forgiven. *(slight pause)* Now have you seen Gabriel? He's a big angel. An archangel.

Wonderful: *(drags in Gabriel, who's ruffling through his script)* Look who I found!

Marvelous: *(recognizes the Angel Wonderful)* Wonderful!

Fantastic: How do we know an angel's wonderful until we've actually heard the angel?

Wonderful: No, that's my name. Wonderful.

Marvelous: Where have you been?

Fantastic: One minute to airtime!

Gabriel: I was busy keeping the planet Mars in its orbit. Seems it was just starting to wobble a bit.

Marvelous: Well, let the other angels handle it. We need you to introduce our witnesses.

Gabriel: *(ruffles through the pages)* Yes, there was something about this in the script. I have to confess I haven't really looked it over too closely. Witnesses to what?

Wonderful: Witnesses to the light!

Marvelous: Witnesses to the light of Christ!

Fantastic: Thirty seconds!

Wonderful: You're to introduce each week's "Witness to the Light," throughout the season of Lent. Each witness will tell her or his story.

Gabriel: I like it.

Wonderful: Good thing, because you're on.

Gabriel: *(looks down)* On what?

Fantastic: Right on cue. Five. Four. Three. *(signals silently with fingers first two, then one)*

Gabriel: Good day. My name is Gabriel, and I'll be your host for this edition of — The Witness Zone....
  Picture this, if you will. A woman of means, desperate for help, sick at heart, sick in her soul, tormented by her inner demons, reaches out in faith to the one physician with the cure. Transformed not only physically but spiritually, she makes it her ministry to support the mission of this one who has come to establish God's kingdom on earth.

When this man, whom she knows as Jesus of Nazareth, is murdered in a judicial travesty, she keeps the faith even in the face of death, and is rewarded by becoming the first person to meet the risen Christ! When she tells others, she becomes the first apostle remembered in all four gospels as the one who proclaims Jesus is risen!

Over the centuries, whenever people tell the story of Jesus to those who know it well as well as those who have never heard the glorious story, they will mention this woman. She is inextricably a part of the gospel story. Her fame is assured.

But here is the irony —

Wonderful: What's an irony?

Marvelous: I think that's what they put in the socket when you're having a knee replacement.

Wonderful: What?

Marvelous: You know. An iron knee.

Fantastic: That's not it at all. An irony is —

Gabriel: Ahem. *(pauses)* Thank you, but here is the irony: A few centuries after this woman shuffled off her mortal coil, a well-meaning Christian wrote a pious fiction about Paul and a woman he called Thecla, a prostitute who was converted by Paul and became an evangelist like him. It was an instant hit, an ancient best seller. People loved it.

And people confused the story of Thecla with the story of a woman named Mary, from the village of Magdala, who came to be known as —

Fantastic: Mary Magdalene! I get it. You're talking about Mary Magdalene. The prostitute who was —

Gabriel: *(thwacks the manuscript)* Mary of Magdala was not a prostitute. She was a rich woman who had a mental illness who was cured by —

Fantastic: Are you sure?

Marvelous: Of course, he's sure!

Wonderful: He's an archangel, remember?

Fantastic: Frankly, I've known a lot of archangels and if you want my humble opinion you can take the whole lot of them and — *(notices Gabriel is watching)* — ah, give them all a raise.

Gabriel: If you're all quite through. *(pauses)* Thank you. So that is the picture we present to you this evening. The story of a woman dedicated to spreading the gospel, whose image has been confused with a fictional character who emerged centuries later. But this is no fiction itself, but the true story, a story we find — in the "Witness Zone."

(Mary Of Magdala enters)

Fantastic: Is that the real Mary of Magdala?

Marvelous: Of course.

Fantastic: And we can afford her?

Wonderful: Might I remind you that this *is* heaven?

Fantastic: Shhh!

Mary Of Magdala: My name is Mary of Magdala. Magdala, otherwise known as Migdol, is the village from which I hail. Mary, or Miriam really, was a very common name in my day. Still is, I'm told. The original Miriam was the sister of Moses, known for singing that little song after Pharaoh and all of his charioteers took a bath in the Red Sea.

Wonderful: I remember that story. I just read it in, just read it in, uh ...

Marvelous: the Bible. Remember? Gabriel told us to read the Bible, and that's in Exodus. How did that song go?

Wonderful: Like this, "Sing to the Lord, for he has triumphed gloriously; horse and rider he has thrown into the sea."

Marvelous: That's right!

Wonderful, Marvelous, and Fantastic: *(chanting)* "Sing to the Lord, for he has triumphed gloriously; horse and rider he has thrown into the sea."
   "Sing to the Lord, for he has triumphed gloriously; horse and rider he has thrown into the sea."

Gabriel: Hey! This is supposed to be a biblical monologue. The definition of a monologue is *one* speaker.

Marvelous: Whoops.

Wonderful: Sorry.

Mary Of Magdala: Thank you. As I was saying, I am Mary of Magdala, Miriam really, named after one of the most famous characters in biblical hist — well, let's skip all that. Since my name was so very common, the Bible finds different ways of distinguishing us, one from the other. There's Mary, the mother of Jesus; Mary, the mother of gospel writer, John Mark; Mary, the wife of Clopas; Mary, the sister of Martha; Mary, the mother of James and of Joses; as well as the other Mary; and that's not counting the Mary whom Paul wrote to in Romans. That's a lot of Marys.

Each of us has something to set us apart, and I am set apart by the name of my village. That alone should have told people that I was a person of some renown, some fame, some, how shall I say it, well, money. I was born into a rich family and I married into a rich family. And a woman of wealth is unlikely to become, well, a woman of the profession that was later attached to my name. So that's the last I want to hear about my being a —

Fantastic: She's a little touchy, isn't she?

Gabriel: Shhh!

Mary Of Magdala: In our society it was very normal and natural for those of us with great wealth to live apart from others, but we were nevertheless expected to perform deeds for the public welfare, such as supporting the arts or paying the way for philosophers and poets. We helped provide what entertainment was available through our patronage.

This was a duty I took seriously, but as the years went by it became harder and harder for me to take care of these responsibilities. I was, to put it bluntly, very, very ill. Possessed by seven demons, I lived in a world of darkness. I rose late if at all, went to bed, struggled with my appetite and my interests, ignored my obligations, and lived, if you can call it living, without hope.

Always, always, I felt listless, without any sense of purpose or drive. People told me to snap out of it, to put on a happy face, to shake off this darkness, and come out into the light, but more and more I found myself seeking the coldest, the darkest room in the house, and shutting the doors against everyone. I drove family, friends, even servants, away from me.

All around me the great pageant of life was proceeding. There were births in town for every death, there were weddings and banquets, feasts, religious holidays, visitors, comings and goings. The crops were planted and harvested, the nets were brought in full into the boats. Life was going on, and it meant nothing to me. I was possessed. I needed help. I could not cure myself alone.

When I could summon the strength I tried to find a cure. I hired physicians of all sorts, some good, some quite honestly fakes, but nothing they tried worked.

Nothing, that is, until Jesus.

One of the gospel writers has told you that Jesus is the light that shines in the darkness, and the darkness has not overpowered that light. One dark day, I heard a tapping on the window shutters. I muttered, telling the people to go away. Go away! But even though I had driven all my family away, there was still one friend who cared about me, and told me something very important. She said something I didn't want to hear, but I needed to receive.

She told me —

Joanna: Mary, you need Jesus in your life.

Marvelous: Who is that?

Gabriel: You'll see.

Mary Of Magdala: — that I needed Jesus in my life.

I had heard about this Jesus, this man who went from town to town, doing more than just curing — he healed people as well. He restored them back into the community of faith.

But you know, I had heard that kind of thing before about other wonder workers, and I knew, they come and they go. There's always a new one.

Still, my friend would not give up.

Joanna: Mary! I know you're in there. Come out. Come out into the light!

Mary Of Magdala: Her name was Joanna, the wife of Chuza, who was Herod's steward. I remembered hearing her case was like mine, very dark and gloomy, possessed by demons, unable to care for herself and others. Now rumors were reaching me that she was doing better, that she had been restored to her family, that all things were becoming as new for her.

Joanna: Mary!

Mary Of Magdala: Go away! I didn't believe her. However, that was her voice at my window. I rose, feeling all the while that the demons were trying to pull me back. And that scared me. If I were truly possessed, if my case were as hopeless as I believed, what had they to worry about? For the first time I had the faintest glimmer of hope.

I went to the door and before I could reach it Joanna threw it open. The light was bright, nearly threw me back, but she caught me, and held me, and dragged me by the hand, ignoring my protests, right into the middle of the town square.

Joanna: Mary, come into the light!

Mary Of Magdala: "Please," I begged her, not wanting to be around so many people, but she pushed her way through, and brought me into the presence of —
 Jesus of Nazareth, king of the world.
 I will never forget his eyes. Old as the ages, young as the first days of spring, deep as Jacob's well, bright as the pools that collect by the road after a sudden squall is driven away by the bright rays of a ravenous sun.
 "Mary," he said, and I never even thought to ask how he knew my name, "your sins are forgiven you."
 At first I didn't know what to make of those words, but suddenly I felt lighter than air, as if I were about to float off on the breeze. I threw my arms around Joanna, begging her to hold me before I flew away. Something was gone, driven away, forced out of my life. The darkness, the demons, were no more. It was brighter than ever, but suddenly my eyes were no longer assaulted by the light. Instead, I felt as if I had been made for this world that surrounded me, as if this good earth had been created out of nothing for me, and not for me only, but all of God's good people who hemmed me in on every side.
 I looked around. Here were the same people I'd always known from the village of Magdala, the widow with the two young children,

the old baker, the teacher of the Bible, and the woman who was always to be found outside the synagogue, praying aloud. Here were the children whose noises I had always hated, and the old people who I feared because I thought of how I, myself, would become old as well. The tanner, who many felt was unclean because he worked with the skins of animals, and the round, fat butcher who gave him the hides of the creatures he killed.

They were all transformed. The children didn't make noise. They sang! The tanner didn't smell from his trade. He glowed with death turned into life. The older people now seemed to me to be pillars of wisdom and truth, every line on their face telling a grand story that is also God's glory.

And Jesus. Always Jesus, at the center of it all. That's when I knew. Jesus is Lord!

Joanna: After that we saw the old Mary we used to know so well.

Mary Of Magdala: Only changed.

Joanna: Well, I should hope so.

Mary Of Magdala: I said earlier that it was the place of rich women —

Joanna: — like us —

Mary Of Magdala: — to support philosophers, entertainers, teachers. Now we had someone really worth supporting. Jesus of Nazareth, the Lord of life.

Joanna: Do you know how much food it takes to feed a hundred Galileans? There are some hefty appetites there, Peter, James, John, those who fished for a living, those who worked with their hands.

Mary Of Magdala: Even Matthew, the tax collector, the one without the calluses on his hands, he had a pretty good appetite, too. I used to kid him about it, but we were glad to do it. Everyone had to eat, didn't they? Besides, it was only money. A few of us had a lot and most had none, but Jesus taught us that we all belonged to each other. I had never been happier.

Joanna: You could see it. She had never been happier.

Mary Of Magdala: That's why I stuck with Jesus — all the way to the cross. *(pauses)* It all came to an end so fast, you know. One moment we were on top of the world, coming into Jerusalem like we did, with the crowd tossing about their hosannas like palm branches.

Joanna: They tossed palm branches, too.

Mary Of Magdala: No one was silent!

Joanna: And remember when he cleared the temple?

Mary Of Magdala: Those who took advantage of the pilgrims, who were selling and changing money on the temple grounds, he sent them packing. We made a lot of enemies that day. Powerful enemies.

There were those who challenged Jesus that week, challenged him with words. He was more than equal to the challenge. "Shall we pay the tax?" they asked. Jesus asked these religious leaders to produce a coin. Instead of so-called pure money, coins with the temple stamped on the front, coins that pilgrims had to exchange their own money for at an exorbitant exchange rate, all they could produce was the money they considered polluted, featuring the face of the emperor. They had intended to trap Jesus, to force him to choose between the religious zealots and those who collaborated with the Romans. Instead, they were trapped.

Joanna: And then it was over.

Mary Of Magdala: I felt the darkness return. I felt the demons crouch at the door. They dragged Jesus away in the darkness, set up a sham of a trial, kept me away from Pilate, where I — and my money — might have had some influence, and nailed him to a cross.

But just when I thought the darkness would overwhelm me, just when I was tempted to go back to my rooms, to hide in the dark, I did the only thing that I felt could save me. I clung to the cross. Here was an instrument of shame, of torture. Here hung the end of the dreams we had shared. But I resolved to live by the words and example of Jesus no matter what happened, no matter what the cost. Others ran. I do not blame them, but we women stayed by the cross.

Even at the end.

Joanna: The next day was the worst.

Mary Of Magdala: The day someone dies is terrible, the wound is wide open and you're in shock. The next day, the first day that dawns with that person absent, forever, is the beginning of the new way, the terrible way of life. That day after they took Jesus down from the cross and laid him in the tomb, was the longest day, the emptiest day. But it was also a day of faithfulness.

Joanna: Then came the third day.

Mary Of Magdala: There we were, in the garden. A new day. A new dawn. An empty tomb. And a message — why do you seek the living among the dead?

We scattered, we women, who had come after the day of rest to prepare the body for permanent burial. We found an empty tomb and a creature of light who told us something we could scarcely believe.

I ran and ran until I found Simon Peter and that disciple whom Jesus loved. I told them, "They have taken the Lord out of the tomb, and we do not know where they have laid him."

Off they went, the disciples, but I was tired, exhausted, and I waited weeping beside the tomb. That's when I saw two angels in white, sitting where the body of Jesus had been lying, one at the head and one at the feet.

They said to me, "Woman, why are you weeping?" I said to them, "They have taken away my Lord, and I do not know where they have laid him."

When I try to tell you what happened next, it sounds like something in a dream. I turned and saw Jesus standing there, but I didn't know it was him.

He said to me, "Woman, why are you weeping? Whom are you looking for?" I thought he was the gardener.

"Sir, if you have carried him away, tell me where you have laid him, and I will take him away."

Then he said my name, "Mary!"

"Teacher," I replied. And it wasn't long before I became the first apostle, the first ambassador for Jesus, shouting in the midst of all the disciples, "I have seen the Lord!"

There's not much more to tell you. I think you know the rest. But there is this — my question — which took me a long time to answer. Why would Jesus pick me? Why would Jesus pick me to be the first one to proclaim the resurrection, the new life?

Think about it. I am a woman. Women were not allowed to be witnesses in court. We were not considered reliable. And my background, the darkness, the demons, made me even less likely a witness.

Shouldn't Jesus have shown himself to the temple authorities, to Pilate, maybe even to Caesar, so that no one would be able to impeach the report?

I know Jesus came to support the weak, the outcast. It was as if God was saying, not by your rules of evidence. Here are my witnesses. Eternal life, real life, is at stake.

It's still at stake. I am Mary of Magdala. I have seen the Lord. You can, too. Just remember, no matter what demons you struggle with, what darkness hems you in, what enemies are arrayed against you, what burden you bear, cling to the cross, that lonely cross, and despite your despair you will know the light, you will know the love, you will see the Lord. Jesus is risen, Jesus is risen indeed!

(Angels all clap)

Gabriel: Say, she was good. Very good.

Marvelous: Thank you.

Wonderful: What a great choice.

Gabriel: But any chance of getting that Jabez fellow? I've been hearing a lot about him lately.

Fantastic: Are you kidding? He's on a book tour. Jabez is out of our price range.

Gabriel: You're on a budget?

Wonderful: This is heaven, not Chase Manhattan. What do you think, that money grows on trees?

Gabriel: But the streets of heaven are lined with gold!

Marvelous: Which means they're about as valuable as regular bricks.

Joanna: You guys want Jabez? Take my advice. Talk to someone with some real cash.

Fantastic: That's a great idea. Mary! Mary of Magdala!

Mary Of Magdala: What?

Fantastic: We were hoping to book Jabez and but none of us seem to have the cash ...

Marvelous: So we were just wondering ...

Mary Of Magdala: I'll think about it. I'll think about it.

Holy Water

Characters
    Youth Group
        Ernie
        Errol
        Earl
        Emmett
        Ellen
        Etta
        Emma
        Eloise
    Two Adult Advisors
        Edward
        Esther
    King David
    Sheep
        Be Bop
        Bo Peep
        Bah Humbug
        Bill
    Piano Player (nonspeaking)

Props
    Luggage with some clothing
    Costumes
    Lyre/harp
    Pull-down screen

Production Note
    This play was written for a youth group preparing to go to National Youth Conference, an event that takes place once every four years in our denomination. The event was still nearly two years away and fund-raising was hot and heavy at the time. The references can be changed to any youth conference or major event for

the purpose of any group producing the play. No tune is suggested for the rap, by the way. The youth enjoyed inventing their own.

(Four male youth and their adult advisor are packing their luggage.)

Edward: Hey, you guys. The van is going to leave without us if you don't hurry.

Ernie: *(yawns)* So what? I'll catch the next van.

Errol: Good luck, Ernie. That'll be in about four years.

Earl: Yeah, Errol, that's how often they have the big Youth Conference. Right, Emmet?

Emmett: Right, Earl. It's no joke, Ernie. Edward, I mean Mr. Evans, is not kidding. If we don't move a little faster, then Ellen, Etta, Emma, and Eloise will leave with Esther — I mean Mrs. Easton.

Ernie: Okay, okay, I'll move a little faster.

Edward: Ernie, Errol, Earl, and Emmett, I'll be right back.

Emmett: Where you going?

Edward: I want to talk to Esther, Ellen, Etta, Emma, and Eloise and make sure they're all packed. *(exits)*

Ernie: My older brother was right. Half the fun of youth conference is the trip out there.

Earl: Fast food three times a day.

Errol: Fries with breakfast, fries with lunch, fries with dinner.

Emmett: And for a snack, more fries.

(Ellen, Etta, Emma, and Eloise enter)

Earl: Hey, everyone, it's Ellen, Etta, Emma, and Eloise.

Ellen: Hi, Emmett.

Etta: Hi, Earl.

Emma: Hi, Errol.

Eloise: Hey, Ernie, where'd you go? What'cha doin'?

Ernie: *(calls from offstage)* Watch this! *(sound of a tub filling with water)* Quick, hand me the Jell-O, there's always room for Jell-O!

Emma: Are you doing what I think you're doing, Ernie?

Emmett: What do you think he's doing, Emma?

Emma: I think he's filling the tub with hot water and Jell-O, Emmett.

Ernie: I think you're right, Emma.

Ellen: What's with you, Ernie? Why would you want to waste water wherever we wander?

Etta: Yeah. Last night at the restaurant you turned a glass of water upside down on top of the tip for the waitress.

Ernie: Wasn't that funny?

Etta: Not to me. I've been a waitress.

Emma: And the night before that it was water balloons. Stop wasting water!

Ernie: Don't be a drip. You can't run out of water.

Earl: What do you mean?

Ernie: How can you run out of water? Every time you want water, all you have to do is turn on the faucet.

Eloise: Sure, you can run out of water. I remember the time the well ran dry on my grandpa's farm.

Errol: What did he do?

Eloise: Stomped around a lot and used a word that rhymed with well.

Ernie: Okay, but that was in the country. In the city all you have to do is turn on the faucet.

Ellen: Maybe you haven't noticed, but things are getting much dryer now that we're getting wet.

Earl: I don't know. It seems to me there's water everywhere. There's too much water sometimes. Ernie's just relieving a little of the water pressure.

(Edward and Esther enter)

Esther: Are you four ready? We've got to get on the road.

Edward: We've got a long way to go until we get to youth conference!

Esther: Say, what's that noise?

Ernie: What noise?

Edward: That noise that sounds like the tub is running. I'll go check. *(walks off)*

Earl: That won't be necessary. Drat! He's gone.

Edward: I just turned the tub off. What was that all about?

Etta: We were just discussing whether it's good to waste water.

Esther: Waste water? There could be some really harsh penalties!

Errol: Like what?

Ernie: Hey, what's happening?

(Some of the others begin to chant, "doodle-oodle-oodle," and wiggle their fingers and their hands go up and down.)

Esther: Oh, no!

Edward: This is very strange!

Esther: I think we're caught in a time warp!

Edward: A time warp? How can you tell?

Esther: Everything is going squiggly and I can hear, "doodle-oodle-oodle," just like Scooby Doo.

Edward: When have you ever seen Scooby Doo?

Esther: I have grandkids.

Earl: Are we going into the past or the future?

Ernie: I hope it's the future. Rocket packs, home helicopters, and personal computers.

Ellen: You don't have to go to the future to get a personal computer. We all have them.

Ernie: I don't. Maybe I'll get one in the future.

Emmett: I don't want to go into the past or the future.

Eloise: Why?

Emmett: I don't want to miss my shows!

(King David and the four Sheep enter)

Errol: Uh oh. Don't look now, but I think we're in the past.

Ellen: Excuse me. Who are you?

King David: Who? Me? I'm the king.

Errol: A king?

King David: *The* king.

Esther: *(points to the sheep)* And is this your court?

Edward: You look like a shepherd.

King David: Okay. Right now I'm a shepherd. But I'm a king. Or I'm *going* to be a king. I've been anointed and everything. Oh, who am I kidding? You've never heard of me. My name is David.

Ernie: King David! Are you kidding?

Etta: We know who you are. We read all about you.

King David: How is that possible?

Eloise: We're from — the future!

King David: The future?

Ernie: Nobody told me there was an echo in the past.

King David: The future? Oh boy, shining armor, jousting, and moats around castles!

Ellen: We're not from that future. We're farther out.

King David: You mean, like jet packs, home helicopters, and personal computers? *(to Ernie)* Did you bring your personal computer with you?

Earl: He's the only boy in the future who doesn't own a personal computer.

Ernie: But I will!

King David: When?

Ernie: I dunno. The future.

Emma: So what are you doing, King David, while you wait to become king?

King David: Right now my court and I are looking for water. Meet Be Bop.

Be Bop: Baaah!

King David: And Bo Peep!

Bo Peep: Baaah!

King David: And Bah Humbug.

Bah Humbug: Baaaaah!

King David: And Bill.

Bill: Burp!

King David: Out here, looking for water is serious business. It's like a desert in the holy land, and every drop is precious. And even though people know better, some are wasters. Do you realize that some people act like water will never end? Out here in the holy land finding water is always a struggle. Can you imagine that some people waste water?

Ernie: Imagine that!

King David: That's why when we write the Bible, we compare God's goodness to water. They're both so precious. When I think of God, I think of water.

Esther: That makes sense. In Genesis, God tames water. God's Spirit moves over the water. God starts the water of the flood, and God stops the water.

King David: That's pretty good.

Esther: I'm a Sunday school teacher.

King David: I could tell.

Errol: So all that stuff about water is really about spiritual things.

King David: What are you talking about? There's no difference between spiritual things and physical things. God's world is one, physical and spiritual. Water is life! God gives life. God gives water. Try living without water.

Edward: So it's all about God's love and God's grace.

King David: You could say that, but it's also about the water. We're all connected by water.

Emma: I read about that in school — how the rainforests and the water and the rivers and the oceans connect us together. What happens in one part of the world affects everyone.

Eloise: And I've heard that many places in the world are running out of fresh water, so we can't afford to waste any of it, or pollute any of it. We have to take care of the world.

King David: God put us in charge of the world, not to use it up, but to be good stewards of it. That includes everything, including the water.

Emmett: Gee. There's not much to do here. I don't see a mall. I don't see a water park.

Earl: So what do you do when you're not receiving visitors from the future?

Ernie: It must be pretty boring out here.

King David: Mostly, I write songs.

Eloise: Cool!

King David: *(holds up harp)* I use my lyre.

Earl: Hey, we brought a lyre along, too. That's Ernie!

Ernie: Wait a minute. I resemble that remark!

King David: Hey, maybe you've heard some of my greatest hits?

Etta: Like what?

King David: Psalm 23, for instance. That one was real popular, went right to the top of the charts.

Ellen: Which charts are those?

King David: The charts for our kind of music. Sheep bop. Hey, let us sing you our song!

Sheep: Bah – bah – bah, bah – bah – ber ann!

Edward: Don't you have to worry about copyright infringement?

King David: How can we infringe on a copyright for something that won't be written over almost 3,000 years?

Edward: Good point. Take it away.

(Sheep create percussion by baahs. King David begins to rap and the others join in.)

Sheep: Bah bah bah, bah bah.
Bah bah bah, bah bah.

King David: I have a shepherd, and he is the Lord.

Esther: Is that true, really?

King David: Really! Word!

Sheep: Bah bah bah, bah bah.
Bah bah bah, bah bah.

King David: He leads me safe by the very still water
I trust in him just like I ought'er

The pastures he chooses have really green grass
I'm safe regardless what comes to pass

How righteous are the paths wherever he takes me
And I feel certain he won't fake me!

When things look dark beneath death's hand
I fear nothing 'cause it's still his land.

There's a great big table
And my enemies are able
To eat all the stuffin'
'cause to my Lord it's nuffin!

Nothing could sever
The two of us, never
And I will live
In his house forever.

Edward: Is that true, really?

King David: Really! Word!

Sheep: Bah bah bah, bah bah.
Bah bah bah, bah bah.

(all applaud)

Ernie: That's great! Just great! So, what's your next hit?

King David: I'm stuck on a new song. It's my 63rd song.

Eloise: Is it also known as Psalm 63?

King David: Yeah, I write so many I have to give them numbers.

Earl: Well, if you're stuck, maybe we can help. Tell us what you want to say.

King David: Here's what I want to say. "O God, you are my God, I seek you, my soul thirsts for you; my flesh faints for you, as in a dry and weary land where there is no water." That's the first verse.

Ernie: Second verse,
 Same as the first,
 A little bit louder,
 And a little bit worse!

King David: What's he talking about?

Etta: Never mind. It's just Ernie.

King David: Got you. But you see what I'm trying to say. Just like in this land, where we faint for lack of water ...

Sheep: We are poor little lambs who have lost our way ...
 Baaah, baaah, baaah ...

King David: In the same way I long for God. I want God in my life. I need water. I need God.

Emma: Which is just the reason we were going to youth conference, anyway.

King David: Youth conference?

Edward: The really big youth conference.

King David: Okay. I'll bite. What's the really big youth conference?

Esther: It's complicated. But mostly it's a place where youth from all over come together to praise God, and sing, and have a good time.

Ernie: Maybe they also come to realize that in the midst of a consumer society where we think we never have enough, it's really God we never really have enough of!

(long silence)

Earl: Was that really you, Ernie?

Emmett: Or did we lose the real Ernie in the time warp and get stuck with the anti-Ernie?

Esther: I want you to say that again, Ernie.

Ernie: Thank you, Mrs. Easton. I'm serious. Listen carefully. Maybe we need to realize that in the midst of a consumer society where we think we never have enough, it's really God we never really have enough of! I was joking about not having a personal computer earlier, but in our family, we try to go without things. We try to spend time together rather than with our things.

Emma: That's deep.

Eloise: Deep as a well.

Ellen: A well full of water.

Etta: A well full of wet water where sheep may safely graze.

King David: Actually, I think that was Mozart, not me. But seriously, you've heard my verse, "O God, you are my God, I seek you, my soul thirsts for you; my flesh faints for you, as in a dry and weary land where there is no water." Do you think you can help me?

Errol: I think we can. Lower the screen, maestro ...

(The screen is lowered and "As The Deer" [Hart] is displayed on the screen. The pianist plays a couple of notes of intro.)

King David: Wow, audio visual. In our school, the closest thing we had to high tech was two rocks with a string attached.

Emmett: Was that like a telephone? Did you use it to talk to each other?

King David: No, it was more like a sling, and I used it to kill giants.

Esther: Oh, that's right. We read about that,

King David: It was in all the papers. Now, I hate to bring up copyright again, but ...

Edward: Don't worry. We paid our licensing fee.

King David: In that case, take it away.

(All — with congregation — sing the chorus displayed on the screen. The Sheep work in an occasional baaah.)

King David: Thank you! Thank you! I've learned a lot about the future. I hope you've learned a lot as well.

Ernie: I've learned a lot. About water, and how we're all connected by it, both those who have none and those who think they'll never run out. And I've learned about God's love, and how we're all connected by that as well.

Edward: Well, I think it's time we go back to the future. We still have a long way to drive today.

King David: Which future are you from, exactly?

Eloise: We're from the twenty-first century.

King David: Early twenty-first century or late twenty-first century?

Etta: Early.

King David: Too bad. You could have gone to the really big youth conference — by rocket. But if you're early twenty-first century you'll have to drive. Listen — be careful with those fossil fuels. They won't last forever. Kind of like God.

Earl: God will last forever!

King David: Of course! God will last forever. God's love is forever. But God's patience ... that's another matter. Anyway, God bless you. And thanks for your help with my song. Good-bye.

Ernie: *(by himself, with fingers wiggling on the ends of his arms going up and down)*
  Doodle-oodle-oodle
  Doodle-oodle-oodle: *(pauses)*
  Say, am I going to have to do this time warp thing all by myself?

Holy Ground

Cast
- Sunday School Teacher
- Sunday School Students
  - Chris
  - Wilson
  - Zed
  - Dusty
  - Astrid
  - Pat
  - Melody
  - Bailey
  - Banyon
  - Fritz
- The Angel Fun
- Grandma
- Dale
- Hungry Person (nonspeaking)

Props
- Bible
- Music (loud, through speakers)
- Tin sheet, pots and pans (to simulate thunder)
- Siren
- Light
- Angel costumes
- Bed or cot
- School chair
- Paper
- Table and chair
- Bowl
- Food
- Clothing

Sunday School Teacher: Class! Class! Welcome. Welcome to Sunday school. This is my first week as your teacher. Actually, it's my first week as anyone's teacher, but since no one else wanted to volunteer, well, it's me.

Chris: Another high-quality teacher thrown to the wolves.

Sunday School Teacher: I hope not. Anyway, today's lesson is from Exodus, chapter 3, about holy ground. Does anyone have a Bible with them?

Wilson: A Bible, what's that?

(laughter)

Zed: Holy ground, what's that?

Dusty: My dad says holy ground is Ketchup Stadium in Pittsburgh.

Wilson: That's Heinz Stadium.

Dusty: I don't care if it's Heinz or Ketchup or V-8 Juice Stadium, on Sundays during the football season my dad stays home from church so he won't miss anything, and all during the game he says a lot of "thees and thous" like out of the Bible, and a couple of "holy moleys."

Zed: So that's holy ground?

Sunday School Teacher: No, no, no. Holy ground is the term that was used when a voice spoke from the burning bush. Moses was told to take off his shoes because he was standing on holy ground.

Astrid: Take his shoes off? I hope he was wearing those gellin' things so his feet aren't smellin'.

Pat: They didn't wear shoes in those days. They wore sandals.

Astrid: But the teacher said "shoes." Who's got a Bible? What does the Bible say?

Sunday School Teacher: Yes, someone get a Bible and look it up. And discuss it please. The pastor sent around a note saying he wanted to meet with the teachers for a couple of minutes. I won't take long.

Dusty: It'll take long enough. Look, can I be the substitute teacher while you're gone? I'm the one with a Bible.

Sunday School Teacher: Well, you can read the Bible anyway — Exodus 3:4-5 — and talk about holy ground. When I come back I want you to tell me the definition of holy ground. *(exits)*

Melody: Oh, great, definitions. The next thing you know, we'll have to diagram a sentence.

Bailey: Somebody read the passage. Exodus 3:4 and 5, I think.

Pat: What page is it on?

Melody: I found it! Here. *(reads haltingly)* "And when the Lord saw that he turned aside to see God called unto him out of the midst of the bush, and said, 'Moses, Moses.' And he said, 'Here am I.' And he said, 'Draw not nigh hither: put off thy shoes from off thy feet, for the place whereon thou standest is holy ground.'" See! Shoes, not sandals. It's in the Bible.

Zed: My Bible says sandals. Your Bible is wrong.

Melody: My Bible is not wrong. This is my grandmother's Bible. Are you saying my grandmother is wrong?

Zed: Let me see that. No look, it doesn't have your grandmother's name on it. It belongs to King James. And what does some king know about the Bible?

Wilson: Forget the shoes. Think about it. A bush that is burning, and a voice speaking out of it! God's voice! That would be exciting.

Banyon: Talk about your special effects!

Wilson: That's just what I was thinking. I'll bet you have to get some sort of special coating so the bush doesn't burn up. And then you could put a speaker so the voice comes out of it. And music. Big music! Loud music.

Astrid: Yeah, but that's not what the teacher wants us to talk about. She wants to talk about real burning bushes, and real holy ground. And God talking out of the bush.

Melody: And I still want to know if it's shoes or sandals. It's important.

Pat: Why is it so important?

Melody: I've got a closet full of shoes and sandals, and believe me, there's a difference.

Fritz: We need an expert. A real expert to tell us all about this story from the Bible.

(A burst of lightning and thunder — noise provided by tin sheet, pots and pans, siren, light — in the midst of this The Angel Fun arrives.)

Zed: Are you...?

The Angel Fun: Am I — who?

Zed: You know, the burning bush and all that, are you —

The Angel Fun: *(laughs)* Hardly! But I do have that effect on people. I'm an angel. Just an angel. Another servant of the Almighty, just like you.

Banyon: A servant just like us?

The Angel Fun: Okay, you don't have the bells and whistles, and you can't fly at the speed of light, nor can you circle the planet Jupiter one second and then whiz down and save a butterfly from an onrushing Mac Truck the next, but if you discount all of those things ... *(shrugs)*

Melody: Sure. Yeah. Just like us.

Bailey: So.

The Angel Fun: So?

Bailey: So, why are you here?

The Angel Fun: You mean, I have to have a reason to just be somewhere?

Chris: Well, yeah. I mean, angels don't just appear out of the blue for no particular reason, do they?

The Angel Fun: Oh, really? And what makes you the expert on angels?

Chris: Well, nothing really. I just thought ...

The Angel Fun: Never mind. It turns out that you're right. I'm an angel, and I'm here for a reason. I'm here to take you to holy ground, just like you wanted.

Pat: Holy ground! You mean, like burning bushes and booming voices. That's pretty scary.

The Angel Fun: What I've got in mind is a lot scarier, but don't worry. You can handle it.

Dusty: Let's go!

Fritz: Just like that? Let's go.

Dusty: Sure. I thought it might be out of this world.

Fritz: Really? And how exactly would we "go" as you put it.

Dusty: Maybe like they do in *A Christmas Carol*, where Scrooge touches the hem of the Ghost of Christmas Past and they fly through the air and stuff.

Fritz: Which Christmas carol? There must be a million of them.

Dusty: Who cares? They're all alike. There's three ghosts and one of them is very frightening. Four ghosts if you count Marley, and —

The Angel Fun: Excuse me. I'm here. Why don't you ask me? And by the way, don't believe what you see on TV. Keep your hands off the hem. These are angel garments, and when it comes time for the cleaning bill there's heaven to pay.

Chris: So how will you take us to see the holy ground?

The Angel Fun: Walk.

Chris: Walk? What's that?

The Angel Fun: It's what you do with those feet that are sticking on the end of your legs.

Wilson: Why do we have to walk? Why can't we have some kind magic or pixie dust or something?

The Angel Fun: Two reasons. First of all, this is the Bible we're talking about, not Peter Pan. And second, you guys don't get enough physical education in high school. When I was your age —

Astrid: Not that!

The Angel Fun: When I was your age I had to walk everywhere, 250 million light years to the nearest galaxy —

Astrid: I know, I know, uphill both ways in the middle of a black hole with meteors raining down on you.

The Angel Fun: How'd you know?

Dusty: One last question. What's your name?

The Angel Fun: My name?

Dusty: Every angel has a name. What's yours?

The Angel Fun: Oh, I suppose it won't hurt you to know. Fun.

Dusty: Fun?

The Angel Fun: That's my name. Fun. I'm the Angel Fun.

Dusty: That's an odd name for an angel. I thought angel names ended in *el*, the name for God. Like Gabriel, Michael, Raphael ...

The Angel Fun: You're right. But Fun-El sounded a little Fun-knee, and I got tired of the other angels talking about me being a funnel for information, a funnel for starlight, a funnel for, okay, you see. So I shortened it to Fun. Any other questions? Now let's go. Hold tight.

(A flash of light and thunder. A bed is brought on stage, with a person lying down, quiet and asleep.)

Banyon: Cool! The other side of the galaxy. So this is what the aliens look like. Kind of like an old person sleeping in a bed.

Chris: What are you talking about? This isn't the other side of the galaxy. This *is* an old person sleeping in a bed. Where are we?

The Angel Fun: At least one of you knows. Or should know.

Pat: I know. Or think I know. This is the nursing home. And that's my grandmother there, sleeping. Don't make so much noise, guys. You might wake her up.

The Angel Fun: Don't worry. No one can hear you right now, or you'd be escorted out in a heartbeat.

Melody: So where's the holy ground? Maybe it's under the bed. Or behind the drapes!

The Angel Fun: Not quite, but this is holy ground and there is a treasure here. Tell me, Pat, why don't you come here to visit your grandmother?

Pat: It's depressing. *(pauses)* Well, this place is full of old people. They can't do anything, and Grandma sleeps a lot. When she wakes up she cries, or asks me questions I don't understand. And I feel bad when I come and guilty when I don't come. It's no fun.

The Angel Fun: That's my name, don't wear it out.

Pat: It's embarrassing.

Wilson: So how can this be holy ground?

The Angel Fun: You want me to give you all the answers? You're all pretty smart. You tell me.

Chris: Maybe she used to be somebody.

The Angel Fun: She still is somebody! On earth all you see is this very tired, very good person! But this is someone who has done great things all her life. And right now, whenever she wakes up, even a little, she's praying for somebody. She's praying for some of you right now. Do you know what a difference that makes?

Zed: Not really. How can it make a difference?

The Angel Fun: Remember the time you were out on your bike and were nearly hit by a truck?

Zed: That was scary. I was just little then. Good thing I was able to speed up just enough.

The Angel Fun: It's a good thing she was praying for you that day. She was remembering you in her prayers, asking for special blessings for you.

Zed: I thought it was me who drove my bike faster.

The Angel Fun: You thought.

Zed: But why would she pray for me? I don't know her. She doesn't know me.

The Angel Fun: Don't you remember those cookies you especially loved at After School Club over at the church? Who do you think baked them? Angels? And she always remembered the way you'd take two or three, and always went for them first.

Chris: So this is holy ground?

The Angel Fun: The holiest. When Satan sees people like your grandmothers coming, he's running. They look weak, but they are very powerful. They've been working their spiritual muscles all their lives long.

Pat: So, you're saying I should visit here more often? But what about the rest of the class?

Astrid: Let's visit *my* grandmother. She's a lot more fun. Mine lives at our home and still makes cookies. She's cool.

The Angel Fun: Yes, your whole class could visit your grandmother. But you could also all get involved at the nursing home. Your whole class could go and sing songs there. You could bring treats. You could adopt residents and write letters.

Fritz: That's a great idea. We could come here once a year and really make a difference!

The Angel Fun: Once a year?

Fritz: Okay, maybe once a month. To start out. And then we'll see.

(Grandma stirs in bed, and sits up. She does not see anyone, except the Angel.)

Grandma: Oh. Oh, have I been sleeping again? The more I sleep, the less time to pray for people I love.

The Angel Fun: And who do you love?

Grandma: *(turns slowly in bed)* Oh, you again. Are you here to come get me?

The Angel Fun: Not yet. But someday.

Grandma: Whenever the Lord is ready. And you ask who I love? I love everybody, or at least I try to. Some people aren't easy to love, but that makes me pray harder. What else do I have left, but love and prayer?

The Angel Fun: What else is there? How is your family?

Grandma: They seem well, when I see them. Of course, they're always in a rush. They come later than they say they will, and they stay less then they promise, but I don't hold them to their promises. I remember what it was like when life seemed all a rush and there wasn't time for anything.

Pat: Hey, Grandma, I'm here! Over here!

Melody: I don't think she can hear you.

Grandma: Life's not easy here, but there are plenty of folks who have it worse. And it seems like I see you folks more and more often which is a good sign.

The Angel Fun: It's a very good sign. Now go back to sleep. You'll need your rest.

Grandma: Any particular reason?

The Angel Fun: I don't know. Maybe you'll be getting some visitors soon.

Grandma: *(laughs)* Not very likely. But it's a nice thought.

The Angel Fun: We'll see.

(Grandma goes back to sleep.)

Astrid: So this is holy ground? Well, it's certainly another world. It's not like holy ground is anywhere near where we live.

The Angel Fun: Don't be too sure.

(More noise and lights. The bed is taken out and replaced with a single school chair, with Dale, a student, sitting there alone.)

Dale: *(begins to fold a paper airplane)* Hey, bay-bee, hey, bay-bee. *(talks to people the others can't see)* Hey, is that supposed to be your nose? I thought it was Mount Rushmore. I thought it was the ski joint. Hey, you're ugly and your mother dresses you funny. Laugh, why don't ya? Don't you know what's funny?

Banyon: Whoah, that's Dale, at the school. This isn't holy ground. This is just the opposite of holy ground.

Wilson: You aren't kidding. I remember when I broke my arm. He said stupid stuff for weeks, inventing different ways he thought I broke it. I can't even repeat any of them.

Bailey: Maybe this is unholy ground, and there's going to be an army of angels coming to cleanse this place. Stand back. There's going to be some fireworks in a minute! *(laughs)*

Pat: That's right! Stand back! You ain't see nothing yet!

Dale: Hey, Bay-bee! I'm talking to you. Hey, Bay-bee! Who cut your hair? It looks terrible. How come your shirt has a pocket? What's in the pocket? Diamonds? Pencils? Is that a plastic pencil protector? Or a lead-lined radioactive pencil protector? Hey. Bay-bee! I'm talking to you.

Astrid: So when do the fireworks start?

The Angel Fun: I'm not laughing.

Melody: Well, you might as well start laughing, because he won't stop, whether you laugh or not.

The Angel Fun: Folks, you're standing on holy ground. Take off your shoes.

Dusty: Look out! Here come the rest of the angels to finish him off. *(pauses)* Honest. *(pauses)* Okay, so there aren't any more angels. Why are we here? There's Dale, and we all hate him because he hates everyone. He's real hurtful. He knows how to hurt people.

Banyon: And his parents won't stop him. They say it's funny.

Bailey: And the teachers won't try anymore. They know it doesn't do any good. He doesn't care what they do to him.

The Angel Fun: Are you saying that here is the one person Jesus did *not* die for?

Chris: *(pauses uncomfortably)* No. But going to the nursing home is sounding better and better. When do we start?

The Angel Fun: Let me ask you a question. Have any of you ever invited Dale to your Sunday school class?

Astrid: Are you kidding? Church is the one place we can get away from him. He's at the football games, he's at the dances, and whenever I go to the store he's there, too, making fun of what we put into the grocery cart.

Dale: Cheerio! Hey, cheerio! What are you, English? Why you putting Cheerios in your basket? Why can't you just say, "Hello," like a normal person. Cheeeerio! Whooo, Whoooo! Here comes the Cheeeerio train!

Astrid: Are you sure he can't hear us?

The Angel Fun: *(a little surprised)* No, I'm not sure. But all the same, do you think he's ever been to any church. Any church? Ever?

Wilson: His parents don't go. I heard his grandmother took him once when he was a little kid but the grownups complained and after a while she stopped taking him.

The Angel Fun: Well, this is holy ground. It's also dangerous ground. I'd like to say that if you invite him to church it'll work out, but there are some things even angels don't know.

Zed: I'm liking this holy ground business less and less. I want to go back to that burning bush thing.

Wilson: Yeah. I'll take off my shoes any time.

Melody: Okay, okay. Let's suppose, just for the sake of argument, that we invite Dale to our Sunday school. What if he says, "No"? What if he comes and makes everyone miserable at church? What if he makes fun of people and they want to kick us out in addition to him?

The Angel Fun: What if? There are no guarantees, campers. That's the thing about heaven. All we ask is everything. Of course, that's all we offer as well.

Banyon: All right, all right. We get it. We'll draw straws and the loser — I mean the winner — will try to invite Dale to Sunday school.

The Angel Fun: Really try.

Banyon: Really try. But first we'll arrange those visits to the nursing home. They're starting to sound better and better.

Dusty: We'll take our youth choir there.

Zed: You've shown us holy ground close to home. How about something a little more exotic, a little more distant? The kind of thing you find in the Bible!

Chris: Something exciting!

The Angel Fun: Exotic? Exciting?

(There is another flash, more sound and lights. Dale's chair is taken away. A very quiet Hungry Person is sitting, hunched over, with an empty bowl in front. He/she is shivering, and barefoot.)

Zed: I guess we're near holy ground, because that person isn't wearing shoes or sandals.

Pat: Quiet. This looks serious.

Dusty: What's happening here?

(Hungry Person moans, and reaches, shaking for the bowl. He/she gazes into the bowl then moan and rolls over, shivering even more.)

Wilson: Hey! Hey! We're here to help.

Astrid: What's wrong? Tell us what's wrong?

Melody: There's no food in that bowl. That person is very hungry.

Bailey: It must be cold there. Look at that person shiver!

Wilson: We can help. Did anyone bring food to Sunday school?

Banyon: You know we're not supposed to bring food. It's not allowed.

Fritz: But we all do. Look, I've got some cupcakes.

Zed: And I've got some candy bars.

Chris: I don't need this sweater. I just wear it to church because I don't want to get my school clothes messy.

Dusty: I'm wearing thick socks. I'll give up my shoes.

Wilson: Hello! Hello! We're talking to you. We've got stuff for you!

Melody: Can you hear us?

(One by one, they toss the food and the clothing toward Hungry Person. The Angel catches the things.)

Astrid: Hey! We're trying to help.

Zed: Yeah. What are you doing?

The Angel Fun: You're seeing someone far off. You can't throw things there.

Astrid: But we want to help.

The Angel Fun: So do I.

Bailey: Then let's work together. We'll give you the stuff, and you fly at the speed of light and take them there.

The Angel Fun: I wish we could, but that's not how it works.

Dusty: What? What good is it being an angel if you can't do things?

The Angel Fun: I am an angel, it's good, and I'm doing things. I'm showing you. This is *your* world. There's nothing you can't do if you set your minds to it, including getting your help to people.

Zed: But how are we supposed to find out where this person is? How can we get the help there?

The Angel Fun: Are you telling me that with all your schooling, your computer skills, the internet, and 24-hours-a-day news you can't figure out where the hungry people are?

Wilson: But it costs money to send things. You could do it for free!

Chris: Why did you show us this when it wasn't possible to help?

The Angel Fun: Who says it's impossible?

Chris: We don't have any money.

The Angel Fun: Really?

Fritz: No, wait. This person here, that's someone who has no money. We've got money.

Chris: I don't ever have any money.

Wilson: You think? Add it up. Think of the money we spend on soda, on movies, on rentals, on just stuff. We've got money.

Bailey: This is not fair. We want to help.

The Angel Fun: It's not fair all right. Nothing about this world is fair, but God is good, and God is counting on you being good as well.

Banyon: We've got to find out where this person is. We've got to help.

The Angel Fun: I think we're getting somewhere. Guys, you've seen holy ground. It's all around you. It's down the street and around the world.

Wilson: The Bible Age isn't over, is it?

The Angel Fun: It's just beginning.

Fritz: Hey, wait! You're not going to leave that poor person alone, are you?

The Angel Fun: Hardly. No one is every abandoned. Ever. *(kneels, takes the hand of Hungry Person, and puts a hand on his/her shoulder)* Hold on. Help is coming. Uh, oh. I think I hear your teacher coming down the hall.

Banyon: You're not afraid of our teacher, are you?

The Angel Fun: Aren't I? Show a little respect. When you're around your Sunday school teacher you're also treading on holy ground. At least around the edge. See you.

(Boom, kaboom, and The Angel Fun is gone, along with Hungry Person. Sunday School Teacher walks in confidently, then stops suddenly, a little puzzled.)

Sunday School Teacher: There's something funny going on here.

Astrid: What do you mean?

Sunday School Teacher: I don't know. Nothing, I guess. Anyway, sorry to be away so long, but I'm sure you've had a good time without me. To tell you the truth, the pastor wanted to let us know something important, though I don't know if you'll be interested. It seems there's been a call for help through our denominational disaster relief for a particular country where the winter is coming on. People are freezing and they're starving, and they need help today, not tomorrow.

Bailey: Freezing? Starving, did you say?

Sunday School Teacher: That's right. They're a long way away, and there are plenty of clothes and food to ship to them, but with the economy in bad shape there isn't money to ship it, and it needs to go right now. They're asking for special donations, but some of the adult Sunday school classes say they've already helped. They said the youth ought to help. Honest, I didn't try to sign you up, but I said that at least I'd ask. Do you think you could —

Wilson: We could all go without soda for a week.

Zed: A month.

Pat: A year.

Chris: And I've got so much extra stuff I was thinking of holding a yard sale. I could donate the proceeds.

Astrid: We could all help.

Wilson: Count on us.

Sunday School Teacher: Well, this *is* a surprise. I was told that the youth didn't like to get involved. We can discuss this more at our evening youth meeting. Now tell me, what do you know about holy ground? Did you have time to open your Bibles?

(Students all raise their hands excitedly, saying, "Me, me, call on me!" Then all freeze and the play comes to an end.)

Considerable Provocation

And let us consider how to provoke one another to love and good deeds.... — Hebrews 10:24

Characters
- Alice
- Erwin (sings a solo)
- Ernie
- Edwin
- Ellen
- Mitch
- Mr./Ms. Winston
- Teacher

Props
- Table
- Chairs
- Mitch's items
    - Earphone
    - Cell phone with internet connection
    - Portable game player
    - CD player with earplug
    - Dark glasses
- Scripts (optional, if play is memorized)
- Backpack items
    - Laptop
    - Video camera
    - Phone
    - Microphone

Production Notes

The play requires a small number of junior high youth. The adults can be played by junior high youth or by adults. Although the youth have been assigned male or female names, you may change the gender of the characters to match your youth group. For instance, Alice can become Alex, Ernie can be Erin, and so on.

The play was written for junior high youth Sunday for the Church of the Brethren in 2005. It was performed in many different churches by both junior high and high school youth. There are references to the recent flood in the Gulf Coast. However, these references can be easily changed to refer to more contemporary disasters. In addition, references to particular denominational offices can be changed to match those of different fellowships.

Mitch should have his electronic connections as visible as possible. I am envisioning one of those earphones that rest on the outside of the ear. Make sure that it rests on the ear that is visible to the congregation. His CD player with earplug, his cell phone, and his portable game player should be very visible. Mitch does not have to be a male. She could be Martha just as easily.

Although an ambitious group of junior high school youth is welcome to memorize the play, what is important is that all are understood. That means they may read directly from the script if necessary. There is nothing wrong with holding the script in the hand. Consider printing the script in a larger font so it is clearly visible so that youth do not have to have their nose in the paper, but can see clearly enough to raise their heads and make eye contact with the congregation. Also, the use of microphones is encouraged.

Youth may choose to make sound effects to go with the "Washington Office Rap." If another member of the group can play piano, then she or he can accompany the hymn text set to "Revive Us Again."

(Alice, Erwin, Ernie, Edwin, and Ellen enter and take their places at a table.)

Edwin: Hey, Alice. Hey, Erwin, Ernie, and Ellen. Looks like we're all here for Sunday school.

Ernie: Almost all, Edwin. One of us is missing, but Mitch should be here any minute now.

Edwin: Let's start the countdown.

All: Five – four – three – two – one ...

(Mitch enters, plugged in and tuned out)

Ellen: Mitch has entered the building!

(Mitch sort of staggers, his hands out groping for a solid surface)

Ellen: He should find a place any minute now.

(Mitch finds a seat and sits down)

Alice: How does he do it? What's he got there? Earphones. Internet connection on his cell phone. CD Player. Game player.

Edwin: It's like being everywhere at once without being anywhere at all.

Ernie: Well, that's about all the excitement we're having today.

(Mr./Ms. Winston enters)

Mr./Ms. Winston: Hi there, all you junior high youth. I've come to tell you that your teacher is running a little bit late. She called on her phone to say she'd be here in about ten minutes.

Ernie: Hey, can I come to your class?

Mr./Ms. Winston: Sorry. You're not in the fifth grade anymore.

Ernie: Yeah, but you always had such neat crafts. What are you doing today?

Mr./Ms. Winston: We're going to build a complete model of the Great Temple of Herod out of toothpicks and popsicle sticks. Then we're going to animate it with holograms and afterward recreate its destruction by the Roman Legionnaires with a couple of matches and some wadded up newspaper.

Ernie: *(to the others)* See what I mean? Fifth graders have the best crafts.

Mr./Ms. Winston: Now wait a minute. You get to do a lot of great things. You had that work camp and the sleepover and the trip to the water park. Anyway, your teacher said to study your scripture and be prepared to talk about it.

Alice: What scripture is that?

Ellen: I remember. It's Hebrews 10:24: "And let us consider how to provoke one another to love and good deeds ..."

Edwin: How do you remember stuff like that?

Ellen: Someone is going to win the Bible Memory Bowl and it might as well be me. Besides, it's kind of intriguing: "Let us consider how to provoke one another to love and good deeds...."

Ernie: What does it mean to provoke someone to good deeds? I thought if you got provoked it was a bad thing.

Alice: What does provoke mean, anyway?

Ellen: It means to anger, incite resentment, annoy, bullyrag, induce, bring about, bother, bebother, bedevil, rub the wrong way, and challenge to action.

Ernie: So if, for example, we were able to provoke Mitch to join the real world then we might bring the scripture text to life?

Mr./Ms. Winston: That's a good example. By the way, how's Mitch?

Ellen: Still plugged in.

Mr./Ms. Winston: *(sighs)* I miss that boy. We haven't talked since he was in the fifth grade. That's when we created the entire Sinai Desert with the sand from our shoes after that beach trip and built a working model of the Ark of the Covenant, hooked up to a car battery to simulate divine wrath.

Edwin: Like I told you. The best crafts. So if our teacher is not here in ten minutes can we come to your class?

Mr./Ms. Winston: Twenty. *(exits)*

Edwin: Okay, it sounds like we've got our work cut out for us.

Alice: What work is that?

Edwin: To provoke Mitch to good works. We can make the Bible verse come true.

Ellen: Good luck.

Ernie: Let's see what we're up against. Okay — he's listening to music on his CD player. That's his left ear. He's got a phone receiver in his right ear. He's got his video game controller in his right hand. And his cell phone has got an internet connection.

Alice: Anything else?

Ernie: He's wearing dark glasses.

Alice: No. What I mean are there any other connections?

Ernie: I think he likes his grandma.

Alice: Maybe we'll get her involved later. She's not electronic, is she?

Edwin: Flesh and blood. She brought the cookies this morning for the fellowship hour after church.

Ellen: What act of love will we provoke him to?

Edwin: I think there's enough suffering from that flood. Let's see if we can get him excited about that.

Alice: *(pulls out her cell phone)* Me first. I know his phone number.

Edwin: What will you tell him?

Alice: Remember that trip we took to the Washington office? How we toured around?

Edwin: I remember. We learned about the influence we have in Washington through our office there, and how we need to think ahead of time if we want to take a stand against war. But Mitch was like talking on his cell phone the whole time to people back home.

Ellen: Do you remember what he was saying?

Edwin: Yeah. Stuff like "I'm in the hallway now. I'm on the stairs now. I'm going through the door now. I'm going to the bathroom now." He didn't pay attention then. What makes you think we can provoke him to love and good deeds now?

Alice: It's worth trying. Okay, here goes. *(enters the number and all gather close to the phone, then she raps)*
    If you ever heard what a real deep cough is,
    Then you'll guess I'm on the line from the Washington office.
    There are people in the world who are down and still suffer.
    And we're the only ones who can act like a buffer.

Between them and the pain of the world that they live in,
Our Washington office can help what we believe in.
We have to provoke all those Capitol people
So they will descend from their pretty white steeple.
And vote to send aid to the ones who are blue.
We stand up to hot shots, like Jesus would do.

Erwin: *(continues)* Mitch, can you hear me? It's you who must reach out.
With help for the hurting as part of this teach-out.

Alice: Mitch, now please listen. I know you can hear me.
We're waiting for answers. Oh my and oh dear me!
We need everybody, can't do it alone.
Mitch, get unplugged —

All: — and get off of the phone!

(Mitch reaches for his ear and takes off the earphone.)

Ellen: He's not listening to his phone. Looks like he's pulling in the internet on that little screen in his cell phone.

Ernie: My turn. My turn. I want to provoke Mitch. Let me see ... I got it. *(reaches into his backpack and pulls out a laptop, a video camera, and a microphone, then turns to face the congregation)* All junior high students carry stuff like this around. *(back to other students)* Okay, do you remember what we learned a couple weeks ago about Brethren Disaster Response? Well, we're going to fake a mobile feed from the Gulf Coast. *(taps a few keys on the keyboard)* I think I've broken into his connection. *(adjusts the camera and all face the camera)* Five, four, three ... *(holds up two fingers, then one, then signals)* We interrupt this website to report on the latest news from Brethren Disaster Response. Weeks have gone by, but the needs are just as great as ever. The destruction is overwhelming, but good folks from around the world are trying to help — including Brethren and Brethren Disaster Response. Isn't that right, Ellen?

Ellen: *(panics)* What? Did you call on me? *(Calms down, speaks in a professional tone)* I mean, yes, that's right. We're reporting from New Windsor, Maryland, the site of the Brethren Service Center, where tons of good stuff gets sent around the world as well as close to home to help people —

Alice: *(interrupts)* I thought we were reporting from the Gulf Coast.

Ellen: Whatever. I'm on a roll. So whether it's health kits and school kits, whether it's a tsunami or a major flood, whether it's a land far away, or our own Gulf Coast, whether — *(pauses)*

Edwin: Whether it's weather or whether it's weathering weather before you wither before it gets worther, I mean, worser — we Brethren are there.

Ernie: With a helping hand, or a hand on a hammer. We've got people on the ground, and the ones not found on the ground are still around through the mounds of cash they've found when they sound the depths of their hearts and sent it to Brethren Disaster Relief. You're never too old or too young to help. And don't forget those junior high work camps organized by the office of youth and young adults at the general board offices in Elgin, Illinois.

Alice: Want more information? Just go to brethren.org on the web. So what's happening out on the Gulf Coast?

Ellen: Let me tell you. We've got folks working with the Red Cross and helping with childcare for those who are filling out federal forms. We've got building crews. We've got tons of stuff getting shipped out of the Brethren Service Center in New Windsor. We've got, we've got —

Ernie: We've got it all, but we don't have you. And that means you — Mitch! We need you to feel provoked about the tremendous need near at hand and around the world. What do you say? Are you provoked to good deeds and love yet?

(Mitch lays his cell phone down on the table, waving his hands in front of his face.)

Alice: We're getting through.

Edwin: But we're not there yet. He's fighting us. Or he's fighting something. I think he's playing the video game.

Alice: Great. What game is he playing?

Edwin: It looks like Doom and Destruction. He's busy waging world war, chilling and killing, slicing and dicing. He's bombing with aplomb. He's shredding, beheading, and deading.

Ellen: Deading is not a word.

Edwin: Maybe not, but it's what he's doing. And it doesn't look very Brethren.

Ernie: What are we going to do?

Edwin: Very simple. It's a little known fact that if we can reach under his player and pull out these two wires ... *(does this)* ... then his game will play in reverse. Let's see, blue wire, red wire?

Ellen: You're pretty sure this won't set off the nuclear self-destruct?

Edwin: Not in *this* game. Here we go. That ought to do it. Now watch. *(Mitch stiffens and holds the game at arm's length)* Right now instead of killing, he's healing. Instead of destroying, he's deploying food supplies to people around the world. Flowers are springing up, while landmines shrink. Baby bunnies and puppies are playing tag. People are packing picnics for after church. Instead of the eve of destruction it's Sunday morning and everyone's gathered to worship God and to hear the gospel of Jesus Christ.

Alice: Sounds a little boring.

Edwin: Must be. He's putting the game down. *(Mitch puts the game down)* We've got him! He's unplugged.

Ellen: No, he's not. He's listening to his CD player.

Ernie: What's he listening to?

Ellen: It's the album, *Annoying Do Nothing*, by the group, Apathy.

Edwin: Mitch! Wake up!

Ernie: Mitch! Come join us!

Alice: It's no use. He's still plugged in and tuned out.

Erwin: *(clears his throat)* Ahem.

Edwin: Erwin! You haven't said anything so far. Do you have an idea?

Erwin: As a matter of fact, I do. We're going to replace his CD with something by the new Brethren group, The Provokers.

Alice: Never heard of them.

Erwin: Is that computer still here? Good. You've never heard of them because they didn't exist until two seconds from now. We're going to record it right now. Where's that laptop? Help me record this song. *(hands out pages to the others)* Join me on the chorus. *(plugs the computer into the CD player — the song is sung to the tune of "Revive Us Again")*

All: When God made the world
    It was put in our hands
    So we might live like Jesus
    Throughout all the lands.

(Chorus)
Hallelujah, we're God's people.
Hallelujah, praise the Lord.
From our building and our steeple
Let us live out God's Word.

We've a message of love
But of strong action, too.
Love is more than just words.
It's the things that we do.
(Chorus)

We can close up our hearts
Let the world ache and bleed
Or like Jesus we'll reach out
To all those in need.
(Chorus)

We have one chance to serve
To come through or else choke.
So to good deeds and love
Let us all now provoke.
(Chorus)

(Mitch starts to rise.)

Ellen: It's working! *(Mitch sits down.)* Or maybe not.

Erwin: We need help. We junior highs are the church, but the church is everybody. We need all of you out there to join with us. We need you to sing along with the chorus. Let's try it right now.

Congregation: *(sings chorus)* Hallelujah, we're God's people.
Hallelujah, praise the Lord.
From our building and our steeple
Let us live out God's Word.

Erwin: One more time!

Congregation: *(sings chorus again)* Hallelujah, we're God's people.
>Hallelujah, praise the Lord.
>From our building and our steeple
>Let us live out God's Word.

(Mitch puts down the headphones and rises.)

Ellen: Hooray!

Mitch: Help! Help! I can't see! *(waves his arms frantically)*

Alice: I help here. This solution is decidedly low tech! *(removes Mitch's glasses)*

Mitch: Guys! Guys! Listen. There's a world of hurting people out there. We've got to get in touch with our Washington office. We've got to send more health kits and school kits to New Windsor. We've got to volunteer to work with Brethren Disaster Relief. We've got to make sure to support all our ministries. We've got to sign up for work camp. We've got to pick up trash around the church parking lot and volunteer to help with childcare and pass out bulletins and start a youth choir. We've got to make things happen in the name of Jesus! There's a world out there! *(pauses)* So what's the matter with you? Can't you see how badly we're needed?

(Teacher enters.)

Teacher: Whew! Sorry to be so late. Car trouble. Have you thought of any ways we can provoke each other to love and good works? *(stops, shocked)* Mitch! Are you all right?

Mitch: Sure, I'm all right. But the world is a mess. It's a good thing we have the gospel to share with others, and that the gospel sends us out in the world to minister in Jesus' name. We've got to do something. But what? Maybe I can get an idea on the internet. *(reaches for his cell phone as the others grab his stuff)* Hey! Hey! I'm provoked. Do you hear me? I'm provoked to love and good deeds. How about you? *(to congregation)* How about you? If you are provoked to love and good deeds, then join me in one last rousing chorus!

Congregation: *(sings chorus)* Hallelujah, we're God's people.
Hallelujah, praise the Lord.
From our building and our steeple
Let us live out God's Word.

Noah's New Ark

Characters
    Narrator (perhaps an adult)
    Elijah
    Noah
    Child One
    Child Two
    Child Three
    Child Four
    Child Five
    Child Six
    Child Seven
    Child Eight

Props
    Chariot of fire
    Footwashing basin
    Sack of groceries
    Power drill
    Construction hat
    Sling
    Styrofoam container
    Apron
    Broom
    Angel cutout

Production Notes

    In this play, Elijah brings Noah back to earth to see if a new ark is needed. He has heard there was a lot of flooding and water at our church. However he discovers that everyone is doing such a great job of serving God that there is no need for a new ark. Everything is just fine!

    The songs I think are ones the children know or can learn. We can always switch the songs. I did not use the same meter throughout the play. Sometimes it is in one meter and sometimes in another. Once the meter changes in the middle of a speech.

You might want a teenager or an adult or two for Elijah and Noah, but perhaps some of the older children might like to try those parts. Otherwise, there are plenty of parts for youth, maybe even more parts than we need. The chariot of fire could be made out of cardboard. It does not need to be fancy.

Narrator: It's two thousand and seven, and of course you all know
That Noah's ark floated a long time ago.
But let us pretend in our own special way
That Noah was building, and building today!

(Elijah and Noah enter in a chariot of fire.)

Elijah: Whoa! Heavenly Chariot! Again I say Whoa!
My name is Elijah, and I'm bringing Noah
Back here to the earth to warn people of danger.
When it comes to boat building, this guy is no stranger.
The way that you act you would think it's a park.
But all of you sinners, get into the ark!

Noah: Thank you, most heavenly chariot driver.
It looks like we're just in time, no late arriver.
I know I once saved all the creatures from water
And only if all of you did as you oughter
There wouldn't be need for the world to take notice
But despite all my warning, you still need a boat. It's
A beautiful world. Would you hear me, you sinner!

Elijah: Forget about breakfast, and lunch, and your dinner.
Last time he saved eight, but this time there'll be fire
And he will save everyone, for I'm no liar.
(changes meter here in midspeech)

80

You boys and girls with your toys and curls
Come into the ark. Come into the ark.
You, cat, you, dog, with meow and bark
Come into the ark. Come into the ark.
Look, I know it's two thousand and seven
But please heed my warning and hold off on heaven.

Noah: The Lord made a promise to hold back the storm.
I heard that you folks had a flood far from norm.
So I as an expert in storm cloud and boat
Came back here to check if your church is afloat.
How good are you people? Should I get my hammer
And build you an ark? Please reply, bark, or yammer.

Child One: *(holds a footwashing basin)* You'll always see me at the church around Easter
That's when I'm a footwasher and a Love Feaster.
This basin's the way that we act like our Jesus.
He was both God on earth and was slave here to please us.
I help to cook the meat and broth and the bread
To show as we worship God's folks will be fed.
We bend knee in service around the whole world.
This is our Love Feast. I am the herald!

Child Two: *(holds a sack of groceries)* I always take the time in both weather foul and fair
To get the food we gather to the pantry over there.
Sometimes our luck is bad or else our job just goes away
When families need a little extra food to last a day
I'm here to take materials donated by our church
We don't want any children to be left within the lurch.
Oh no, I think we all have known how hungry hunger feels
And that is why this church insists we help to make their meals.

Noah: The horses they champ in the general warming
As animals gather against all this storming.

Child Three: *(holds a power drill and wears a construction hat)*
These tools are just a few of what we used after the flood
That left our basement full of dirty water, filth, and mud.
The smell was bad, and even those with stomachs strong said, "Yick!"
But that was for a moment. Then these tools we all would pick
And after that we worked quite hard to make our basement better.
This is our church. There is no way we'll leave it wetter
Than the stream that winds its way beneath our city.
By working hard we all made sure that everything is pretty!

Children sing "Rise, And Shine, And Give God The Glory, Glory"

Child Four: *(has one arm in a sling)* The pastor's like a captain who helps navigate our ship,
But all the rest of us can help us gather in worship.
I lead the choir as I must. I wave my broken arm
Which lends to hymns and anthems what they call a certain charm.
Sometimes I sing, sometimes I pray, sometimes my hands I'll clap.
Whatever way that I can help. If someone takes a nap
Throughout the sermon I can see that this one still gets sleep
But later I can give a tape of worship she can keep!

Children sing "The B – I – B – L – E, yes that's the book for me.

Noah: Come into the ark while there's still a chance.
Don't pause for a change of clothing or pants.
Come into the ark, though it won't be pretty
When the waters are covering all of the city.
You saints and you sinners, still out in the park
Pack up your picnic. Come into the ark.

Children Five and Six: *(together hold a styrofoam container)* We sometimes feel tired, but at least we still can move.
There's some who hold the church within their hearts and love
The people here, yet they are sick, or tired, or very old,
Or worry they might break a hip when it is icy cold.
So though we never blow a trump or make a lot of fuss,
We like to take a greeting to these folks from all of us.
It doesn't take a lot to take the Spirit dwelling here
And bring it with a smile to some other folks out there.
Next time you feel out of sorts, we'll tell you what to do!
Just visit folks who can't get out. You'll both be happy, too.

Children sing "Stop And Let Me Tell You, What The Lord Has Done For Me."

Child Seven: *(wears an apron and holds a broom)* I'm one of the youth. Though I may look dyspeptic
It's only because right now life is so hectic.
There's so much to do, whether music or sports,
Or just doing homework. I get out of sorts.
But when I was told there were homeless to feed
I got in the car — which is just like a steed —
And went out to Washington, Columbia district,
To help with the homeless. It's fun, it's not this strict.
Setting tables and serving and cleaning up after
Then sleeping on floors, making noise, raising rafter,
No matter how much that I try to accomplish
We're here to serve Jesus, by sweeping and wash dish.

Noah: Come into the ark. The rain from above
Is a warning to fools from the author of love.

Child Eight: *(holds angel cutout)* There is an empty pew or two. That's clear from any angle.
But that's because we sent to heaven more than one good angel.
These very special people, saints in heaven and on earth,

Who by the way they lived have proven just how much they're
  worth.
They're like the yeast in bread dough, rising high, they act like
  leaven
And when they're through they do their best to drag us all to
  heaven.
They do this twice, for first of all they show us their behavior
And then of course we won't forget they say the Lord is Savior.
We miss them all of course, and many times have shed a tear
But these are folks in heaven. That's forever, folks, I hear.

Noah: What think you, Elijah? They've had their harsh flood.
  There's no need for deluge. These people are good.
  The rainbow's in the heavens, and the promise we can keep
  That summer, spring and, harvest time when all good people
    reap
  Will follow one another.

Elijah: And don't forget the spring!
  I loved the way the children raised their voices, let songs ring!
  Let's gather all the cows and sheep with this, our happy lariat.
  And then the two of us can once more hop into this chariot.
  We'll fly back up to heaven where the city is a park.
  These folks are just too good, my Noah. They don't need an
    ark.

Noah: We'll leave things alone, and we won't flood them out
  Instead we will listen while all the kids shout!

Children sing "I Am A Christian"